BOWL

First published 2006 by
Worple Press
PO Box 328
Tonbridge
Kent TN9 1WR

British Library Cataloguing in Publication data.
A catalogue record for this book is available from the British Library

ISBN 1-905208-09-X
ISBN 13: 9781905208098

Worple Press is an independent publisher specialising in poetry, art
and alternative titles. **Worple Press** can be contacted at:

Worple Press
PO Box 328
Tonbridge
Kent TN9 1WR

Tel: 01732 368958
E-mail: theworpleco@aol.com

Worple Press gratefully acknowledges Arts Council support

Typeset and printed at Peepal Tree Press

Elizabeth Cook

BOWL

for Viv and Peter

Thankyou for your kind
hospitality! what a lovely
place to be

Elizabeth

10 vii 10

worple
press

CONTENTS

for Helen

A bramble caught hold of her skirt, and checked her progress. Instead of putting it off and hastening along, she yielded herself up to the pull, and stood passively still. When she began to extricate herself it was by turning round and round, and so unwinding the prickly switch.

Thomas Hardy, *The Return of the Native*

BOWL

Give me a bowl, wide
and shallow. Patient
to light as a landscape open
to the whole weight
of a deepening sky.

Give me a bowl which turns
for ever on a curve
so gentle a child
could bear it and beasts
lap fearless at its low rim.

BEES ON BEES

The difference between
your fingers straight, side by side, like a wing,
and when you open them, letting air in
to the space that a web might fill.

So the pussy willow,
like small gold bees, their bright aureoles
a shimmer of pollen lifted,

and the swarm of snow flakes
that the air was busy with all night:
fat bees silently moving, to land – each cell intact,
nothing packed down –

to rest so gently
on each willow bud, balanced on uncrushed stamens.

THAW

Yesterday I ran for the first time
in almost a year. Downhill
admittedly, and I was late
for an appointment, but the running
was not from anxiety, just a sense
of pleasure in opening the throttle
and moving after months
of being careful, lying, sitting, walking
only in measured stages.

                     The street
was a suburban row but it tipped
down into the distance, like a road
that leads to water.

                     Today
I assayed the bicycle.
It needed some oil, but was soon
moving swiftly enough and freely
along the towpath by the canal.
There everything is beginning:
knobs at the ends of branches swelling
into green; the two swans
who negotiated last month's ice
with hauteur, now use their beaks for dredging
the soft silt under them. One comes up
festooned with a streamer of green weed.
I imagine their great black feet
pushing away the water
as they cruise, scouring the banks,
looking for somewhere to build.

REAL LIFE

An old woman, dressed probably in black,
sits outside in the sun. Feet shoved
into flat slippers, her thick legs
placed wide apart. Her lap is wide.
And on her lap a large round tray,
or possibly a sieve. And she rests
her well-used hands upon the sides,
and the tray or the sieve or the bowl rises and falls
gently with her breath.
Now she could easily pass whole days
going over each grain on this full tray;
her body no more than a light
balsa-wood frame
for remembering, marvelling.

EAST LIGHT

Brightness pours out like a snow of blossom,
a blizzard of bone, wind-shaved.
Hard to stay
just in the here
when the fields leak a pale must bloom
and the full sea is troubled
by the streets and by the churches it overflows.

Hills are burial mounds;
shadows sharp:
each body has one, each moving beyond now,
lessening and growing, by a means like the jelly
that forms round germinated seed, or the halo –
at first no more than a thought –
of green at the edges of March trees.

Suffolk, April 2002

Keats and Virgil

On the day you heard of your mother's death you took refuge
in the box of air beneath your teacher's desk,
refused to come out of the exiguous place
which nursed you so imperfectly.
Schoolmaster now your mother and father –
did he manage to coax you from that kennel with titbits,
milk of fine phrases
to get your own mouth round?

We know he fed you Virgil.
Did those well-placed, tight-packed words
cause you to climb that very desk
and plant your flag like a conquistador?*
You must have been avid for it. What healthy boy
translates the whole *Aeneid* after school?
How, having done it, could you lose it?

> *(I remember a man in Pentonville Prison
> ask could he stand and read out loud,
> John Donne's *Death be not proud.*
> When those words
> moved through that other body,
> the slight Geordie thief
> became for some moments a tall man,
> filled out, made straight, articulated.)

We do not even know
how your English *Aeneid* began. *Arma virumque cano*
turned over and over like a conker
in your pocket till you found the word
to speak out first.

Arms, man, and, I sing.
My song is weapons and man. *A* man? Keats
or Aeneas first?
Weapons or song? I guess

if even a small fragment remained – a syllable
might be enough to grow the rest out from.
Like skin, when a piece the size of a petal
builds cell on cell to form a fresh
acre of living tissue,
or in a single flake of paint is found
true azure of the Virgin's gown.

the fountain

The fountain remembers, yesterday
her waters formed a fleur de lys
and all her past
is fleur de lys, though now
winds blow the drops astray.

And rivers run through her
and guttered rain
and melted snows. The molecules
are not the same, though every one of them recalls
its predecessor's form.

Thread

Sometimes she'd be on a roll, catch
at spindrift that spooled out around her,
discover a sturdy thread, and ride on it.
Exactly like Jean Gabin,
Or, *Did you find us easily?*
They all come unstuck at that beastly dogleg.
Those who knew her, knew the riffs, might travel
a short way with her,
each riff a jetty, or the angled deck
of an aircraft carrier, launching her further
into the unprintable air.

Sybilline

Life is that property of matter
whereby it can remember. And memory works
by metonymy. So a small remembered piece of poem –
its action though *no stronger than a flower* –
may yet restore a contiguous neighbour
(as here the rhyme prompts *power*).

Here's a morsel of leaf –
so slight a scrap an ant
could transport it as a parcel.
Suppose it the last
identifiable fragment
written on by the Sybil:
carefully, with tweezers
we'd lay it on a bed of muslin,
display it in a monstrance.

The Sybil offered Tarquin nine volumes of her scriptures.
The price was high and he refused to pay it.

So she burnt – or maybe ate – three of the volumes
and offered the remaining six
at the same price. Again, more emphatically perhaps,
he turned them down. She destroyed three more.
And so on, till at last he paid the full
initial asking price
for a piece so tiny
and torn it was wholly
illegible.

as in amber

The young mammoth was so perfectly preserved
it made one of the team cry,
as if she had lost a beloved pet and found it, caught
at the moment of death. If love
could revivify this woolly creature
then her love would. It could not.
But in its stomach were undigested grains –
recognisably wheat – that might sprout yet;
and in its mouth, half undestroyed,
was fern like maidenhair, its small spore still
on the underside of the leaves the hungry beast
had recently ripped from the growing bush and was chewing
when the avalanche pounced upon and held him.

HEART OF STONE

It's an effort for the bus to make this journey.
It wheezes on the turning roads that
one hour's drive away from Florence
are now its only way. Now
wherever we stop – by a building
or worn path – as someone climbs down
the engine dawdles; when we go on
there is a kind of yearning
for those diminishing figures
making their way home
down a track they know. No one gets on:
the process is one of shedding.

By the time we reach Vallombrosa
there are only three others. We all get off
and the bus turns round.
The next one back to Florence
leaves in five hours time.
It's started to rain.

I make the decision to walk –
it's the trees after all
I have come for; those whose leaves,
turning in the air as they none-the-less fell,
made Milton think of rebel angels, cascading
turbulent from heaven.
It's late October. Many have fallen –
chestnut and beech; only the firs
remain green.

The narrow path I climb is shiny
with fallen leaves. I have to watch my step.
As leaves drop onto me I think
not of Milton but a story
I liked as a child where a poor man,
unable to buy a gift for his friend,
went out leaf-catching. He caught three
hundred and sixty five gold ones
and bagged them in a sack,
earning himself a reputation for lunacy,
giving his friend an entire year of joy.
I catch a leaf or two but most elude me.

This place has been a kind of goal,
somewhere I'd promised myself
before leaving Italy. Was it only the name
I was after? Val-
ombrosa. A name cleft naturally.
How to translate
ombrosa? 'shady' or 'shadowy'?
The valley of the shadow.
Now I've arrived my heart is heavy
though rain or no rain
it is as beautiful and umbrageous
as its name (and indeed
this deciduous beauty
is founded on rain).

Climbing this path
(so narrow – *stretto* –
there's no room for two)
I feel uneasy, as if someone

were breathing behind me, urging me on,
making me stumble and fall. The valley below –
beautiful, yes, in gold
and red – but also,
this gorge rushing down to my left,
ravenous.

I make it to a wider ledge.
There, secure behind bars of iron,
a recumbant figure cut in stone.
He's propped up on one elbow
like someone reading in bed,
but instead of a book there's a cross.
The inscription overhead
says here Gualberto tussled with devils
who threatened to fling him
down the ravine. Mercifully,
a rock mollified and let him in.
There he entered the stone's soft heart
and hid till the devils gave up.

Suddenly I'm hungry. I've only
two apples in my pockets: I eat them both –
pips, core, even the woody stalk – then turn
to pick my way back down the slope.
Careful, but the dread has gone.

The monastery gates are open.
Someone's been doing the laundry:
white linen tumbles
from an upstairs window
and the sun beats it dry.
There's no one about;
only the bees make quiet forays
from their village of hives.
Like the brothers who tend them
their work is within.

I enter the chapel
and at the threshhold dip
my fingers into the stone font,
seal my brow with icy water,
feel the cool of whitewashed stone
slip over me like a silk gown
and sit, sheathed in silence,
while beyond, birdsong
(rare in this land of hunters)
cases the silence up. Green
presses on the clear windows.
Grass, fir, the unfallen
foliage, and ferns crowd outside.
Its presence felt first as a silent
wash of verdure, then
more clamorous, till the whole chapel
thunders with soft green flame.

THE KINGDOM

The first lookout was the Bramley tree,
shaped kindly for a timid child – foot-hold,
hand-hold, seat – as if the branches were moulded.
Even I, who felt safe virtually nowhere, felt safe there
perched on the high bench I'd made my throne.
But my kingdom was not the apple tree
or the surrounding garden and land I could see from there.
My kingdom was simply myself and the apple tree
helped me to take possession.

Nearly twenty years later, in a frenzy of agitation,
I set off across a snow-draped orchard –
a creature whose purposes are hidden
even from itself, driven only to move, seek
the nutrient it lacks.
I found a hospitable tree, climbed up into it and stayed
till my mind settled like the snow and I saw
that the planned marriage
must not take place. (He came to find me, said
I looked like a huge vulture perched there
in my brown fur.)

At Ichok I look down
on the backs of eagles, the brown shingles
of a farm roof an hour's climb below.
The air so thin here nothing gets in the way:
it illuminates like clearest water (as, swimming,
you'll see pebbles far beneath in all their lustre).
I can see further now
than ever before. It is suddenly evident

that what the soul longs for most is freedom
and that our particular prayers for the dead, naming them,
may hold them back. The dead want us
to let them go.
As I prayed for them –
you – my beloved dead –
it was as if I cut each bird
free of its jesses; watched it circle,
circle wider. Then fly away.

I can remember but not sustain
the vision at Ichok.
Now when I think of Chaucer's Troilos
it's not of laughter from the eighth sphere
but his tenderness for earth –
this 'litel spot'
embraced by sea.
Standing again on high ground,
Scotland at my back, North Sea to my left and England
like an apron before me,
I love what I see; I want to be free
in it, not of it.
A startled pheasant rises from low gorse,
heavy wings whirring
like the blades of a wind-up toy. She lands
twenty feet or so away, and returns
to her tranquil inspection of turf.

FARM

seven: When my parents went away
I stayed at the farm in the valley
where my friends Hugh and Julia lived.
By day we ranged and grazed on cowcake,
sucked and gnawed the hard green nuggets,
denser than pemican.
We burrowed in haylofts, making rooms
and corridors between bales,
jumped in the pit
of smouldering sileage.
At night their mother
shimmied our clothes off,
bundled us three
into one hot bath.
There we ate oranges.
The juices dribbled freely down chins and arms
into the scummy water.

ten: Same farm but different family.
I think this mother less reckless
than Hugh and Julia's.
Clare is ten like me –
at school we call her Dolly
on account of her bubbly hair.
We make a sedate progress
up the steps to the low slide;
we look after little Sarah
and splash each other politely
with the inch of temperate water
carried out of the house in a milk pail
to the paddling pool on the lawn.

The rest of the farm is out of bounds.
One evening that summer Clare and Sarah
were killed by their mother. She shot them in bed –
did they wake first? – then shot herself.
Their father was eight miles north with his lover.

thirteen: Janey Greensleeves lives here now.
I got my guinea-pigs from her
(they breed like rabbits).
One night there's a party: boys,
girls and cider. We talk about scrumpy –
how they chuck rats and all sorts into the vats.
Protein, says Alan, *the acid breaks it down*.
We pretend to puke but keep on with the Merrydown.
There's a swimming pool sunk in a field. Not blue-
painted sides and chlorine. Just a hole like a tank
with a concrete lining.
The water has warmed all day in the sun.
It is dappled and marbled
with effluvium of cattle.
That night we took our clothes off and jumped
into the soupy water.
Bumped and bobbed, reached
body against body, not quite sure
what hardnesses and softnesses were what
or whose. We climbed out stronger,
our bodies filmed with slime.

TO, NOT FROM

The teacher lifted my comfortable man's
cardigan with a disdainful finger.
It was regulation beige
but the length offended her.
'You look like a hippy', she said,
having already kept me late for lunch
on account of another thing I'd done wrong
or been wrong. (There was so much of that
in those days, I forget.) I remember my heart
swelled as I thought, in words,
'You have nothing to do with me.
Why do you think
I mind what you think?' Then I thought,
They didn't put bars
on these windows. The doors
aren't locked. Why do they think
we'll stay here?
Is it some kind of mass hysteria
that keeps us all within bounds,
eating our meals at delimited times,
arriving for lessons or games, then returning
for prayers and the bedtimes they've set.
When I got back they were all eating lunch.

I went to my room and tugged from the wainscot
my father's pigskin holdall.
In it I put my treasures:
photos of friends,
a phial containing strands of saffron;
and I changed out of uniform beige and tweed

into clothes that I favoured: a deep
purple blouse, a velvet bolero;
a long, elegant black skirt
like Bonnie's in *Bonnie and Clyde*.
I hung silver stars and beads like the dew
round my neck, from my ears;
and I loosened my hair from its brown
ribboned bunches, brushing it free.
Then in the hush of communal dining, I walked
through the unlocked door
out to the path and from there to the road
where I fed on ripe blackberries.
A Romany drove the van I flagged down.

Since then I've done it again
once or twice, when confinement
required it. And some
shake their heads in dismay
at this habit of running away.
But listen instead to the runners:
watch as they tell,
as their limbs become fluent,
tongues inexhaustible, remembering the taste
of the moment they knew they were more
free than anyone thought. And know
that we run not away from but to,
as Christian (though his wife and children
cried after him) ran on,
his fingers in his ears, calling
'Life! life! eternal life!'

CAT AND HEN

They're at it again. Spindle
the cat and the fat
hen from three gardens down meet
in next door's yard to spar.

So evenly matched: at a weigh-in
I reckon there'd not be two ounces
of difference. Bulk for bulk the conical
and the cylindrical square.

Putty to play with. *There's*
your blob. What'll you
make? Whiskers? A tail?
My one's got wings. What's yours?

The cat prances forward. The hen
totters backward, beating her wings
in modest withdrawal. O what
a hullaballoo!

He pounces. She rises, her wings
give her succour. Astonished
(again) he sees that she's up there,
somewhere between the sun and his head.

Pugilist or suitor? Always
he fronts her. So Peleus
held fast to the ur –
form of Thetis

though she tried to
dodge him. Fire
into water; lion, then snake; ink-
fish (spilt over). Hold on! Be true.

Bam Bam: Stone. Bam Bam:
Scissors. Bam Bam: Paper.
Bam Bam: St.... Got you!
My paper wraps your stone.

Again he covers
the wall's ridge. She mutters
oblivious. He lands
neat before her.

Will you have me, lady?
No my lord. Impasse.
Come on.
Try again.

TWO EXPERIMENTS

i. man and fish

Chuang-tzu and Hui-tzu
look down at the River Hao.
Minnows are swiftly
threading the waters
this way and that,
never colliding.

'See how those minnows
dart as they please',
said Chuang-tzu
to Hui-tzu,
'In this resides
the happiness of fish.'

Hui-tzu answered, 'How
— not being a fish —
can you know such a thing?'
Said Chuang-tzu, 'You're right
to use the word *How*
and concede that I know.

Let me show you my means:
I stand thus by the Hao,
look down at the water,
take note of the fish,
happily darting
wherever they please.'

ii. man and dog

René Descartes nailed
his wife's dog to a tree.
The dog howled piteously.
Madame Descartes wept.

From such experiments Descartes concluded
that a dog is without a soul.

CLASH

When we meet it's the clash
of humming birds:
long tongues driving
through close tunnels
to nectar pooled
at the flower's throat.

Nectar or lava? Sweet gathering
of dew or a dip with the tip
of the tongue into Stygian hot pepper?
AAAH that flavour!

                When you move
and I move it is tight
as blades making love; wired
light of foil points:
hard to say who follows,
who leads, who blesses,
who wounds.

                And what air
upholds us, or by us is whirred
into light in our swift,
unaccountable, dance.

EDWARDIANS AND BIRD-HEADED MODERNS

They wore hats, open as platters,
with dead birds on them
and artificial fruit. Their corsetted
torsos and faces suggest
ignorance of the carnage they carry.

                                        But these

are worse who wear birds – live ones –
incorporated into their heads. Sometimes
a whole copseful is there: jays
and magpies and starlings
(not thrushes or robins) they bray
their conflicting demands out for food
and perch. Six thousand
and eight disharmonious
voices say 'Mine', stabbing
the air with their beaks and angry
scuffling of wings.

                                        The slightest

thing sets them off to scatter
like gunshot has scared them.

                                        I once saw

a whole flock of starlings rise
squabbling from one single mild
woman's head. I would like,
very quietly, to steal up
and net them, and free them
as far off as the Amazon.

RAID
(*Iliad* x)

Of course it is true: there were horses,
swift and keen as the Black-Sea
winds that stirred them to swiftness
and keenness; manes white
as the snows on Rhodope. Whiter.
Of course it is true that Diomed and Odysseus
needed to take them from Thracian
Rhesus, knot reins together
so they'd move as one team
then, whacking them, loose them
into the hot night.
True that Odysseus for once
stopped thinking as the sight
and thunder of those moon-
pale horses
took his breath away, nearly.

Some left though for whistling
low to Diomedes, busy with tackle.
Make him look up.

ASH

Last night I dreamt of a man, tall and calm as an Ash tree,
asleep in my bed, and me
sleeping, and waking
warmed by the stern length of him
stretched out beside me.

DAWN FIELD

I want to remember this:
all the grass bound and covered with cobwebs;
small baskets, cat's-cradles, dew-wet, white in sunlight;
like linen on hedgerows, or an encampment –
like the Field of the Cloth of Gold in silver.
A whole field ready, laid out with snares.

THE TWELVE DEGREES OF LONELINESS

(i.m. Edward Arthur Cook 1869-1914)

'It has occurred to me',
wrote my father in his diary,
'that the subject of loneliness, in all its forms,
offers more scope to a writer than any other.'
(Tripoli, 1960)

i. Beacon

Not quite an island: a promontory
that reaches like an arm into the sea,
a lighthouse at its farthest point
and you in it
fighting to keep awake
during the long watches.

There you darn socks,
shake remedies into new potencies
and make note in your journal of the waves –
their colour, texture, intervals and volume –
and how the seabirds ride.

ii. Kuala Lumpur, May 1914

I see it as a ledge in a small garden
– a terrace that gives the impression of far reaches.
Dipped out of the view of the house
where no one else lived my grandfather
sat in the reclining wicker chair
where sometimes he'd sat, with drinks, among friends.
This time he did not recline in the chair.
He sat hunched, head hung to the left
where he looked in despair at the naked ground
and saw it stare back. From his right pocket
he took the small gun that had hung so heavy,
skewing his jacket,
and for some moments cradled it,
cherished it at his breast like a wounded bird,
himself huddled round it, comforting it.
Then he carried the dear thing up to his mouth –
or was it his temple or brow?
I imagine the brow, dead centre
– oh grandfather –
it was nothing like the red thikka of honour.
It shot you to buggery.
Further from home than ever.

iii. Bullet

Small, hard, harmful thing,
ninety years on, still travelling.

Having ploughed through my grandfather's skull, you flew on,
skimming the Himalayas;
briefly got tangled in a prayer flag
strung up like bunting
above a white rush of water
that spills down Kanchenjunga
(a small piece of his tissue dislodged there to dance
in the sky-sieved spume like a ball in a fountain,
acquiring some merit)
while you – the original,
the hateful bad object,
never-dissolving suppository – kept going,
riding the thermals
 – the Urals, Constanza
(the swallows, gathered
like beads on an abacus,
shivered with the cold
breath of your passing).
You sped over the Danube,
skirted Sarajevo
(oblivious of the blizzard
of your kin to be born there,
the blood that will tunnel
the snows of next winter),
over gleaming Mont Blanc,
to the Somme, then home
to the England whose lead and antimony
composed you in Kynoch,
Birmingham. Here,

unspent, you linger;
scorch yourself in
to the grain of his children.

Aristotle said dreams were like small frogs
travelling in the fluids of the body,
or (I say) like the plastic toy
submarines of my childhood, packed tight
with a charge of sodium bicarb to rise
in the bath with quiet
poppings and fizzes.
So you, irreducible particle,
nightmare-carrier,
persist in our blood
where your mute detonations
continue to burn and freeze.

iv. My Giraffe

My giraffe
has a huge heart,
strong enough
to pump aired blood
as far as his high head.
He feeds on eucalypt and rowan —
the tallest trees here in my garden.

I hope that if he stoops to drink
he will not raise his head too fast
and faint.

v. Bubbles

The beginning of that visit is so like the end
I cannot divide them. Going up to the house,
looking in through the fogged-up window
to see you moving on the other side,
gently as a moon-walker
bobbing and dancing a slow T'ai Chi
at the end of his line.
Already almost unreachable.

But we pressed in through the steam of vegetable water
as if through a jungle of lianas and screeching macaws,
or as if we were all underwater,
not swimming, but wading with the weight
and burden of water mutating each gesture
so that words came out and dissolved like the soft
bubbles from a baby's mouth.

vi. I'll bleed to death if I want to

After he had vomited a river of blood
they poured in twelve pints more
and fed tubes into him.
One of these flared into two balloons,
inflated to push on the walls of oesophagus
and duodenum. A pair of suffocating water-wings
to press the blood back in.

That night, in the hushed ward,
he rose from his bed like the Kraken,
stood tall as a house and with more hands
than the nurse had ever seen on one man before,
began to drag out those tubes.
Plunging his hands clean through the veil
of enough sedation to stun a horse,
to haul, if necessary, his insides out.
Strong as Samson when he groped for the pillars,
working blind but with whole will,
he searched the deep bath, scrabbling for the plug.
Drowning in blood, he wanted
to let it out.

vii. Longing

The times you stood her up:
the leg of lamb,
the salmon trout,
summer pudding and a full
carton of cream
waiting in the larder,
because you'd said you might come down on Friday
or if not Friday, Saturday
or maybe just – at least –
arrive for Sunday lunch.
Then something would crop up,
something to worry her –
yet again you'd got most awful 'flu
(*he really did sound dreadful*)
and all you could do was crawl into bed with Lemsip.
Who did you think you were kidding?

To her, two gaping days
– everything else got out of –
to sit under the apple tree
or in winter by the fire,
and search her heart, longing.

Longing for you since the day
she set out from Liverpool Dock
on the Elder Dempster Line,
the memory still warm
of the perfectly beautiful baby
in her arms. It grew warmer
all the way to Lagos

till it burned.
                And you, frozen,
no more able to take a step
than the baby lifted from her arms
could have crossed the widening gap
between the ship and shore.
(Lately vodka's numbed the pain
till the windows steam up.
Only a tiny splinter stays sharp
and refuses to go away.)

Now that the black sea
has eaten her again
you're back on the quay of the dock
searching the frightening dark
where the sea slaps and the boats
knock against the sides.
This time you reach. This time you are able
to fetch what is needed in order to move.
Clumsily, fearfully, but with all your heart
you hurl yourself after.

viii. Now as it narrows

Now as it narrows there is still more room than you ever thought possible.
You make your way through the avenue of lime trees,
find doorways of light keep pace with the shadows,
offer long views onto summer and birdsong.
Distance and leisure; you almost stroll
to the one path you know, to the house you remember,
into the hall where the tall window's panes
cast a pale aquarelle of ruby and sapphire
across yellow floor tiles.
Do you run up the stairs to the landing where the books wait,
their spines a soft mesh where for years fingers hooked them?
or into the drawing room – the piano is open,
a Haydn sonata in C dur where she left it,
the music still ringing – which way did she go?
Into the dining room? - fruit on the sideboard -
or the cool scullery where ferns crowd the window?
Did she leave by the back door for applemint or thyme?
Choose it, go after; run down the flag stones,
past the woodshed, past the remains of the bonfire.
Now you're running, I can hear your feet thud on the earth path
as you follow surely calling *Mum, Mummy, Mum.*

ix. You

You'd just gone home
when the nurse told us he wouldn't last the night.
So I ran to the station, hoping the train
would not already have come and gone
taking you with it.
I saw you first, a dark figure
wearily moving across the bridge
that spans the two platforms,
and I saw that the other was the one we'd each
least choose to be left with;
and I knew that by daylight there'd be no one left
on the earth who'd be dearer than you.

x. A Child's Grave in Volos: 450 B.C.

Little girl, I hope you will not
be lonely in this small place.
Your dolly is here by your side
and a comb. You can play
combing her hair.

Will you be warm enough?
It's pure wool
the purple shift they made for you. And look!
a second pair of shoes for when
you've worn the first ones thin,
and a tight hat
when the sun's glare or the beat
of the rain insist.

You won't go hungry.
This basket's filled – nuts,
an apple, a pomegranate –
filled to show you what to do.
When it's empty
you must put on your sandals and go:
gather more in.

xi. Snow

Throughout the day, snow
at the edge of my gaze.
Your shocked mind
frozen behind the blizzard.

I fear I may grow snow-blind;
hope for soft rain.

xii. Cut Edge

Everything has changed shape.
The old fence ripped down, the new
malletted hard in.
The little lawn I'd worked the ground for –
de-stoned, sieved,
raked, seeded and watered –
is now beyond the pale.
It looks to me – this new fence –
like a row of pike staves
with the raw severed heads
of friends rammed onto them.
Seeing them caught in their last agonies
it is hard to remember
the sound of their laughter.
Here was a revolution.
First there is slaughter,
then the re-drawing of lines.
There are cabbage stumps everywhere
and a chaos of splinters and seed.

ABISHAG

1 Kings i, 1-4

The King was asleep when they brought her,
covers heaped over him. She didn't get in,
just lay there, naked as they sent her, on top of the furs.
The King never stirred until, chilled by the morning,
a dry hand reached over the covers to feel her,
then absently stroked her, twitched her towards him
as if fondling a pelt or a favourite dog's ear.

JUDAS TREE

I tasted a flower today,
sharp and liquid
as a sour berry.
If I were thirsty
I might graze on whole branches.

Did you have name before Judas
hanged himself on your naked wood?
Or blossom before you extruded
the stricken pink flesh of his loathed body?
Did your leaves deform into hearts out of pity
for the unloved, un-prayed for?

BIRD

Of one thing we can be sure: that *BIRD*
is at the heart of this language.
The letter *BIRD* signifies 'bird'
but *BIRD* as phoneme is an element of many
poly-syllabic words (giving,
to the untrained mind, an irrresistible
suggestion of birdsong). Long labour,
the discernment of pattern and rhyme,
allow us to assign meaning
to three hundred and eighty five words
and a putative grasp of verb forms.
We can also surmise that birds (the creatures)
were greatly revered in this culture (viz *I* in ours).
One unusually extensive fragment
contains eighty three instances of *BIRD* on its own
and great clusters of the letter *BIRD* in phrases.
We think this a hymn or a recipe. The letters are well formed.
This fragment also uniquely contains
the single instance of a letter whose value
we as yet do not know. The letter is shaped
like the head of a spear, or a leaf that is cordate.

PHILAE

After the hot, stinking, blood-
blinded waters,
where the severed, scattered
parts of Osiris
thrash for remembrance,
here is a laving.
On rocks the white linen,
knuckled by sunlight,
stands back from the threshhold of all quickening.
Columns are folding
day into shadow.
Here in this room
set within like a casket
the table is scrubbed;
here she begins her methodical labour
lit by a single
snake of green water.

GEB/NUT

Tonight I'll be Nut, cover
the earth so my belly's
the tent of the sky.
You be Geb: earth below me,
your cock the lone tree,
a stick to paint
stars on this canopy.

I'll be earth tomorrow:
drink rain from you.

LET ME...

Let me put it in you, please —
he said: like it was a piece
of proved dough
ripe for the oven, or a potato
hot from the cinders
to warm her cold hands on.

IN THE NIGHT

Half waking in the night, you cry out
whimpering like a cowering boy or a very old
demented man. Before I frame
myself in kindness and reach out,
I think, mercilessly,
'Is this what it's going to be like?'

DISSOLVE IF YOU WANT...
from Eugenio Montale, *Ossi di Seppia*

Dissolve if you want
this whimpering scrap of life
as a sponge wipes out the ephemeral
scribblings from a board.
I am awaiting my return into your circle;
the journey's finally done.
My coming bore witness
to an order which escaped me as I went;
these words of mine pledge faith
to an impossible event of which they know nothing.
But whenever I have caught through other sounds
the soft rakings of your waters on the shore
a sense of disturbance took over
as when a man draws a blank when he tries to remember
the land of his childhood.
I have taken what I know
less from your evident
splendour than from the breath that barely
breathes a sound as it stirs in the wastes of midday.
I give myself to you humbly. I am no more
than a spark struck from the Reveller's wand.
But I do know this: that in burning,
in this, nothing else, is my meaning.

THE THINKING REED IN FOG

He never could resist an empty bottle.
In the days when wine was only for high-days
I would wait till the bottle was empty and watch him
as his eyes widened with interest and pleasure
at what seemed an idea he'd just made up.
He'd pick up the bottle, pucker his lips,
breathe down – not blow – like a flautist at the rim
of his instrument, breath steady as the sound,
unearthly, bloomed.

'Foghorn calling through the channel' was what he'd say.
Always he would say this, always
do it, and always it would feel a good, original joke:
to make the sound which was not
his breath, not the hollow glass, but the one
as it moved through the other;
a stirring of life I attempt now, pushing
the grain of the mist and the fog,
the squalls and the years aside, to sound the obscure channel.

TO GREG AT THE FAR END OF HIS FATHER'S LIFE

Today you look very small
and the air around you, endless
as the air that wraps a child.
You've practised the words of the Kaddish
and the turquoise Indian shawl
you wear with such panache
sits quiet now as a prayer shawl
as you wait, obedient, scared
for your forefather's mantle to slide
from the upper ledge, heavy as snowfall.

SENSE

You ask how I,
a hundred or so
miles away, know
you're in love.
It's simple. Imagine
you're carrying two corners of a big sheet,
your arms stretched out.
Someone else grasps
the other two corners
making the sheet taut, like a tarpaulin
to catch the dew.
Then the other lets go.

SKIN

Thank you God
for my skin
which keeps the world out and
me in.

BLISS AND VEGETABLES
Numbers xi

I find it hard to long for unitive bliss
when what I miss
is you, and you, and you.
So the Israelites tired of the manna which fell with the dew,
tasted of honey, dissolved in the sun.
They wanted the fish, leeks and cucumbers of Egypt.
The strong taste of onion.

CAP FERRET

Twelve each: like small rock pools –
the greys, the duns, the lustre,
their craggy exteriors.
A low January sun:
lemons and pale wine. The fact
that the oysters are living makes the act
more personal. Like taking you
into my mouth or tasting
my salt on yours.

WHY I DO NOT FEEL READY TO LEAVE THE WORLD OF SENSE

1. Because when I studied mathematics I took great pleasure in problems
   involving baths and the radii of plugholes and taps. I was attracted
   to the idea that you could verify the results
   obtained from an algebraic working out
   of how long it would take to fill or empty a bath
   whose taps were x cm across and whose plughole y cm
   and whose own depth (up to the overflow) was z. It pleased me
   that it would be possible to construct a bath of these dimensions
   (and though I couldn't do it, such a thing could be done
   in the world of matter where people are skilful) and to fill it
   and empty it
   and see.

2. Because when I look at the small, purple, gold-rimmed tapering glass
   on the table in front of me, a pale, delicately-pronged
   yellow and cream aquilegia, next to a spray
   of raspberry-pink weigela whose dark green leaves
   are ribbed and veined with yellow, the pleasure
   these colours and shapes provide
   is so great I cannot
   contain it.

3. Because eternity is in love with the productions of time.

4. Because when I was eight I read a book
   called *Flaxen Braids* in which there was a girl
   whose cheeks looked 'as if a drop of cochineal had fallen
   into a bowl of cream.' This was my first conscious
   experience of metaphor. It dropped
   into me and spread,
   slowly, like the cochineal,
   pooled at the centre and widening
   into a reticulum of tiny veins.

I wanted to find a bowl from the kitchen and fill it
with the yellow clotted cream my mother and I
walked five miles to Roecombe each Thursday to fetch
then watch what occurred when I dropped in the red
(which I'd heard was from ants' blood) which we usually used
to make white icing pink. I wanted to be there at the centre
of the fine suffusion which – were it not contained by the cream bowl –
could stretch to the ends of the earth.

POPPIES

Poppies, fine as air-
mail paper,
open their cups
wide and wider,
till cups turn to saucers.

They follow the sun
as it moves round the garden,
receiving the light which fills
them to breaking.

SHADOWS AND ANGLES

A dream of convergence.
Me in the apple loft, you outside,
high on the ladder, looking in at the window.
Your shirt is open – I can see the delicate
ridge of the clavicles, their shallow gradient
to the hollow at your throat.
The shadows and angles in this:
apple ladder,
acute at the top like an easel;
the dark where it leans by the wall, and the wide
generous angle your bones make, almost meeting.

INTERRUPTION

In the middle of the night, a hush
like the pause between the in-
breath and the out-breath of the tide.
After the rake-out, sucking at shingle,
a silence, chaste, as birdsong gathers
before the swell.

AT MONTERCHI
(the Madonna del Parto)

Layer on layer has fallen away or been driven.
Now two strong angels part the heavy curtain.
Look where she fingers the gash in her gown –
it's slit from heart to womb
and white chemise peeps through.

Tug that out and you'd see
flesh of drum-tight belly,
and below, where lips part –
opening to womb and heart –
as the child's head presses.

WATER

Since you, images of water. Dream
of a tidal wave, poised to annul me
while I waited in creaming waters.

Nights by rivers, white noise
that roared us to sleep, filled us
with liquid currents, pooled splendours, till we
were every mountain stream, all snow-melt, joined
into one broad irresistible water
breaking in silver fire.

Water at your feet that laps and idles
like a tide still undetermined
where the main pull is.

Downpour all day. Rain is all the verbs,
all puissance, rushing in lines.

ACKNOWLEDGEMENTS

My thanks to the editors of the following publications in which some of these poems first appeared: *Agenda*, *Moving Worlds*, *The Shop*, *Stand* and *Tears in the Fence*. 'Bowl' was also printed accompanying Mali Morris's paintings in *Slow Burn: Meaning and Vision in Contemporary British Abstract Painting*, 1998.

I am grateful to the Estate of Dame Lucie Rie for permission to use a photograph of her bowl on the cover and to Kay Poludniowski of the Sainsbury Collection, University of East Anglia, for her help in supplying it.

Lastly I would like to thank my editor, Peter Carpenter, for his support throughout the making of this book and for providing an ear I trust.

NOTES

p.16   *became for some moments a tall man* Joseph Severn recalled that
'Keats was called up into grave manliness at the mention of anything
oppressive and seemd like a tall man in a moment'

p.18   *Life is that property of matter....* Samuel Butler, *Life and Habit*,
London, 1880

p.24   *Ichok* in the Nepalese Himalayas

p.29   *as Christian...* in *The Pilgrim's Progress*

p.30   *Peleus... Thetis* Ovid, *Metamorphoses*

p.32   *Chuang Tzu...The Complete Works of Chuang Tzu*, New York,
1968, pp. 188-189

p.61   *Philae* in Egypt, dedicated to the cult of Isis

p.62   *Geb/Nut* in Egyptian iconography the male Geb represents the
earth, while Nut, the sky, is female and is represented arching her
body over Geb who lies supine beneath her, his erect penis reaching
up towards the heavens.

p.65   the Italian original 'Dissipa tu se lo vuoi...' is printed opposite
Jonathan Galassi's translation in Eugenio Montale, *Collected Poems
1920-1954*, New York, 1998, p.78
(The Italian word *tirso* clearly means *thyrsus* though translators seem
to have ignored this.)

p.66   *thinking reed* Descartes' phrase *le roseau pensant*

p.77   *At Monterchi* Piero della Francesca's pregnant Madonna, the
Madonna del Parto, stood in the chapel of the cemetary at Monterchi
(where it is likely that Piero's mother was buried).

Worple Press is an independent publishing house that specialises in poetry, art and alternative titles.

Worple Press can be contacted at:
PO Box 328, Tonbridge, Kent TN9 1WR Tel 01732 368 958
email: theworpleco@aol.com.

Trade orders: Central Books, 99 Wallis Road, London E9 5LN
Tel 0845 4589911

TITLES INCLUDE:

Against Gravity – **Beverley Brie Brahic**
(A5 Price £8.00 ISBN 1-905208-03-0, pp 72)

Full Stretch – **Anthony Wilson**
(Price £8 /10 Euros ISBN 1-905208-04-9, pp 104)

Sailing to Hokkaido – **Joseph Woods**
(A5 Price £6.00 ISBN 0 9530947-6-6, pp 60)

Bearings – **Joseph Woods**
(A5 Price £8.00 / 10 Euros ISBN 1905208-00-6, pp 64)

'his work shows an impressive reach and range' *Eiléan Ní Chuilleanáin*

'good and interesting poems well-presented' *Books Ireland*

A Ruskin Alphabet - **Kevin Jackson**
(A6 Price £4.50 ISBN 0 9530947-2-3, pp. 88)
'you may like to consult *A Ruskin Alphabet* by Kevin Jackson, a collection of facts and opinions on ruskin and Ruskinites, together with a variety of pithy remarks from the man himself' *TLS*

Looking In All Directions – **Peter Kane Dufault**
(A5 Price £10.00 ISBN 0 9530947-5-8, pp. 188)

'Wonderful stuff'   *Ted Hughes*

The Great Friend and Other Translated Poems – **Peter Robinson**
(A5 Price £8.00 ISBN 0-9530947-7-4, pp. 75)
Poetry Book Society Recommended Translation

The Verbals – **Kevin Jackson in Conversation with Iain Sinclair** (A5 Price £12.00 / 20 Euros ISBN 0-9530947-9-0, pp. 148)

'Highly interesting.' *The Guardian*
'Cultists will be eager to get their hands on it.' *TLS*
'Worple Press have done it again... this sparkling introduction to Sinclair and his world.'   *The Use of English*

Stigmata – **Clive Wilmer**
(A5 Price £10.00 / 15 Euros ISBN 1-905208-01-4, pp. 28)

'a brilliant piece of work which brings honour to our time'
Sebastian Barker

FORTHCOMING TITLES

Buried At Sea — **poems by Iain Sinclair**

To be In the Same World — **Peter Kane Dufault**

Warp and Weft — **an anthology of Worple writing**